ideals®
AUTUMN

The miracle of fall renews
My faith, and I'm reborn!
Triumphantly I take my stand
This bright September morn.

The spectacle of beauty
In leaves of red and gold
Against the denseness of tall pines
Is wondrous to behold!

Fields of pumpkins cast
Their orange reflections in a stream.
Soon gentle hands will harvest them
For faces that will beam.

The smell of caramel apples
Now permeates the air;
And ducks gather near cattails,
Their flight plans to prepare.

The coral blush of western sky
Caused by the setting sun,
Strengthens the glow I feel inside
Just knowing we are one.

Wendy Wagner Tousignant

Editorial Director, James Kuse

Managing Editor, Ralph Luedtke

Associate Editor, Colleen Callahan Gonring

Production Editor/Manager, Richard Lawson

Photographic Editor, Gerald Koser

Copy Editor, Sharon Style

An Autumn Landscape

Brilliant scarlet and crimson stain,
  And splashes of yellow gold,
Warm brown stubble and ripened grain;
  The waysides seared and old;
A dazzle of green where the aftermath
  Breathes a tale long told.

Gray where the haze hangs over the west,
  Blue where the asters grow;
Purple the lights on a hill's far crest,
  The shadows mauve below;
Blackbirds wheeling above the corn,
  Silent, serenely slow.

Lights and shadows and sparkle of wine,
  Somber color and gay;
Rich and warm in the late sunshine,
  Chill where the shadows play;
Thus God hangs His masterpiece
  Over the world today.

Grace Noll Crowell

ISBN 0-89542-326-X 295

IDEALS—Vol. 36 No. 6 September MCMLXXIX, IDEALS (ISSN 0019-137X) is published eight times a year,
January, February, April, June, July, September, October, November
by IDEALS PUBLISHING CORPORATION, 11315 Watertown Plank Road, Milwaukee, Wis. 53226
Second class postage paid at Milwaukee, Wisconsin. Copyright © MCMLXXIX by IDEALS PUBLISHING CORPORATION.
Postmaster, please send form 3579 to Ideals Publishing Corporation, 175 Community Drive, Great Neck, New York, 11025
All rights reserved. Title IDEALS registered U.S. Patent Office.
Published Simultaneously in Canada

ONE YEAR SUBSCRIPTION—eight consecutive issues as published—only $15.95
TWO YEAR SUBSCRIPTION—sixteen consecutive issues as published—only $27.95
SINGLE ISSUES—only $2.95

Work!
Thank God for the might of it,
The ardor, the urge, the delight of it—
Work that springs from the heart's desire,
Setting the brain and the soul on fire.
Oh, what is so good as the heat of it,
And what is so glad as the beat of it?
And what is so kind as the stern command,
Challenging brain, and heart, and hand?

Work!
Thank God for the swing of it,
For the clamoring, hammering ring of it,
Passion of labor daily hurled
On the mighty anvils of the world.
Oh, what is so fierce as the flame of it?
And what is so huge as the aim of it?
Thundering on through dearth and doubt,
Calling the plan of the Maker out.
Work, the Titan; Work, the friend.
Shaping the earth to a glorious end,
Draining the swamps and blasting the hills,
Doing whatever the spirit wills—
Rending a continent apart,
To answer the dream of the master heart.
Thank God for a world where none may shirk;
Thank God for the splendor of work!

                    Angela Morgan

"Work" by Angela Morgan is reprinted by permission of DODD,
MEAD & COMPANY from THE HOUR HAS STRUCK.

Arithmetic

Arithmetic is where numbers fly like pigeons
in and out of your head.
Arithmetic tells you how many you lose or win
if you know how many you had before you lost or won.
Arithmetic is seven eleven all good children go to heaven
—or five six bundle of sticks.
Arithmetic is numbers you squeeze from your head to your hand
to your pencil to your paper till you get the answer.
Arithmetic is where the answer is right and everything is nice
and you can look out of the window and see the blue sky
—or the answer is wrong and you have to start all over
and try again and see how it comes out this time.
If you take a number and double it and double it again and then
double it a few more times, the number gets bigger and bigger
and goes higher and higher and only arithmetic can tell you
what the number is when you decide to quit doubling.
Arithmetic is where you have to multiply
—and you carry the multiplication table in your head
and hope you won't lose it.
If you have two animal crackers, one good and one bad,
and you eat one and a striped zebra with streaks all over him
eats the other, how many animal crackers will you have
if somebody offers you five six seven and you say No no no
and you say Nay nay nay and you say Nix nix nix?
If you ask your mother for one fried egg for breakfast
and she gives you two fried eggs and you eat both of them,
who is better in arithmetic, you or your mother?

Carl Sandburg

Home Canning—
Its Rewards and Delights

Canning begins at our house in mid-July when the cucumbers are ready. It ends in late September or early October after the last juicy tomato has been packed into a hot quart jar, and the final batch of applesauce has been blended with cinnamon, cloves, nutmeg, and ginger and packed away to be enjoyed some dreary winter day.

The fruits and vegetables won't wait. Unanswered letters are stacked in a drawer; half-finished novels are returned to the library for another time. Beginning with dill pickles, we try to obey both the letter and the spirit of the old saying, "twenty-four hours from vine to brine."

My husband and I have been canning for several years, and as soon as our three sons could safely hold a paring knife we enlisted their help as peelers, pitters, slicers, and choppers. The boys know how to scrub cucumbers to remove all the sand between the bumps; they know which tomatoes to put into our bushel baskets as we bend over the rows of a pick-your-own farm. They remember to drop the peach pits in a separate bowl, saving them to use later in the pinecone wreaths we make.

Best of all, the boys recognize those glorious smells that are part of home canning. They have whiffed fresh dill. They know it's bread-and-butter pickle time when the pungent, sweet-sour smell of turmeric, celery seed, mustard seed, sugar, and vinegar comes to a simmer in the huge pot on the stove. They know, too, that once you've tasted a home-canned peach you will never again be satisfied with the store-bought variety.

I cannot think of many experiences more satisfying than home canning. True, it's hard and sometimes tedious work. The kitchen gets mighty warm when pots of water are boiling for hours at a time; and there are moments when one medium-size cucumber looks just like another, and another, and another, each waiting to be washed and sliced. The rewards, however, are immediate. After the last quart jar is removed from the steaming kettle and set alongside others on the kitchen table, we heave a contented sigh. We may talk about this year's yield as opposed to last year's, or wonder how many new jars we'll need next year; but subconsciously we're listening for that delicate, almost musical *ping* as each jar cools and seals. Sentences are chopped into fragments as someone cries, "There goes another one!"

After the jars have cooled overnight, they're ready to place in brilliant colored rows on wooden shelves in the fruit cellar. Pints of mustard pickles stand in front of their taller dilled relatives. Crimson tomatoes rub shoulders with jars of blushing peaches—plain and spiced. The always dependable applesauce stands next to this year's experiments: carrot sticks, cauliflower buds, green pepper rings, and small onions, all pickled and waiting to be served as surprise hors d'oeuvres.

Canning is a delight not confined to taste and sight, for canning is a friendly, sociable pastime. I cannot imagine canning by myself. Friends have joined us to slice onions, chop green peppers, and stir the brine until it comes to a boil. Their reward? Several beautifully packed jars, tied at the neck with red or green yarn and placed under their Christmas trees.

My husband was raised in a family where canning was done as much out of necessity as out of personal pride. Food was "put by" on that remote farm in northern Wisconsin against an often cruel and unpredictable winter or as insurance against next year's possibly poor growing season. I'd be willing to guess that it's those memories that have led him to stand patiently at our stove, dipping wire baskets full of peaches or tomatoes into boiling water, then carefully slipping the skins away from the fruit. He streamlined the bread-and-butter pickle process, too; he found that after the pickle, onion, and pepper slices had soaked for hours in salt and cracked ice, they could be efficiently drained in an old pillowcase hung from a pipe over the laundry tubs. Even the basement smells like pickles!

My own memories center around jams and jellies. Because my mother raised seven children before, during, and after the depression, she learned nothing if she did not learn thrift. I remember her standing, night after night, stirring huge pots of fragrant purple liquid that would become delicious Concord grape jam. It was a sure sign that I was growing up when I was allowed to pour the hot, melted parrafin—oh, so carefully—on top of the shimmering jars of jams and jellies. The ultimate treat, of course, was spreading a thick layer of jam on a slice of warm homemade bread; my mouth still waters at the thought.

Despite the abundance of processed and pre-packaged foods today, people are returning to home canning in astonishing numbers. Manufacturers have trouble meeting the demand for jars, lids, and rings. Perhaps, in a way, we're looking for the old values, the old realities. Certainly a case can be made for the economy of canning one's own fruits and vegetables, but I suspect the motives go deeper than mere price. There is something undeniably rewarding in picking, cleaning, and canning those gorgeous products from the summer garden. There is pride, and a sense of accomplishment, and the unabashed delight in being able to say, "Isn't it marvelous? I canned it myself!"

Bea Bourgeois

Countryman's God

Who reaps the grain and plows the sod
Must feel a kinship with his God:

For there's so much on earth to see
That marks the hand of Deity.

When blossom springs from tiny shoot,
When orchard yields its luscious fruit,

When sap is running from great trees,
On all occasions such as these,

The man who breathes fresh country air
Must know full well that God is there.

Roger Winship Stuart

Fall Apples

The apples hang heavy on the branches now,
Bright scarlet, and mellowed by the sun's warm glow.
Fall's rich yield is everywhere
On the hill where the orchard sweetens the air.

I lose sight of the barn and the weathercock,
The stubbled fields where the summer grain was shocked.
For the trees with their heavy-laden limbs
Merge their branches and leaves and hedge me in.

I see with delight where apples lie on the ground,
Checkering the rich earth in scarlet and brown;
Where apples cling loosely to every stem,
And I have acres of trees to find the best gem!

At last, the apples I seek are ripe,
Sweet and crunchy and delightfully right;
Not like the one that once puckered my lips,
Green and stone-hard when I bit out a chip.

But off I must go to spread the word,
To the wren on the post, past the grazing herd,
To Father in the barn, lifting hay from the mow . . .
At last, the apples are ready to be gathered now!

Joy Belle Burgess

Big Chief's Prayer

Great Spirit,
Hear me
While I offer the united voice
And devotion of thy people
In thanksgiving.

For the sun
That warms our earth-house,
Filling it with all good things.

For sleep that rides
With the moon and stars;
The rivers that flow
From mountains
Of living water.
For healing herbs,
Fruits, nuts, grains,
Fish, and meats.
For the spirit of the hunt
When the great chiefs smoke
The pipe of peace.

Keep us the children of nature,
Tall, erect, strong,
Brave, and young.
Teach us the patience of the turtle.
Give us the vision of the eagle.
Give our prophets wisdom.

Teach us to love our Mother Earth
With her dawn,
Evening light, dark clouds,
Mists, trees, flowers,
Seeds, and corn,
And the rains that come
From the Thunderbird.

Make us humble
Before the great mystery
And worthy
Of our ancient faith.
When the fires die out
And the winds no longer blow,
Lead us down the beautiful trail
To the camp of our fathers
In the Happy Hunting Grounds . . .
So may it be, Great Spirit,
So may it be.

Samuel Harden Stille

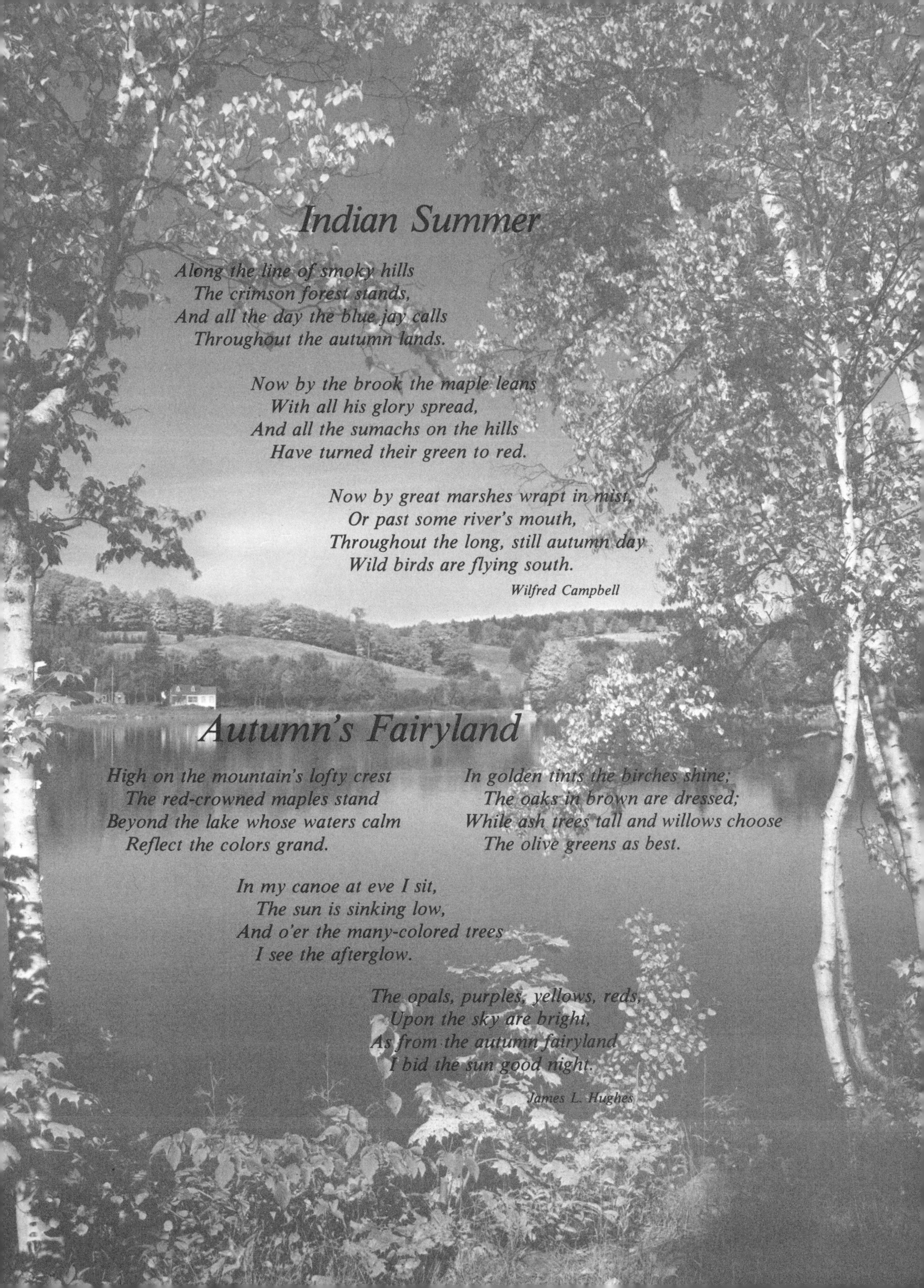

Indian Summer

Along the line of smoky hills
The crimson forest stands,
And all the day the blue jay calls
Throughout the autumn lands.

Now by the brook the maple leans
With all his glory spread,
And all the sumachs on the hills
Have turned their green to red.

Now by great marshes wrapt in mist,
Or past some river's mouth,
Throughout the long, still autumn day
Wild birds are flying south.

Wilfred Campbell

Autumn's Fairyland

High on the mountain's lofty crest
The red-crowned maples stand
Beyond the lake whose waters calm
Reflect the colors grand.

In golden tints the birches shine;
The oaks in brown are dressed;
While ash trees tall and willows choose
The olive greens as best.

In my canoe at eve I sit,
The sun is sinking low,
And o'er the many-colored trees
I see the afterglow.

The opals, purples, yellows, reds,
Upon the sky are bright,
As from the autumn fairyland
I bid the sun good night.

James L. Hughes

The Taste of Freshly Made Molasses

Everyone in the family had work to do at molasses-making time; but nobody objected because each one of us knew that the tasty delights of Mama's molasses goodies were worth working for.

Long before frost time, Papa would carefully carve seven wooden machetes (with handles that wouldn't leave splinters in little hands) used to strip the leaves from the sugar cane. Each of us was carefully instructed to strip each stalk clean and to remove every trace of the dried leaves at the base of the stalk.

When we finished stripping the entire field of leaves, it always reminded me of a forest of green fishing poles. The next step was to cut down the stalks and remove the seed heads. No one but my brother John, however, was allowed to help Papa with that job because it called for the use of sharp corn knives.

Afterwards, the cut stalks were corded into neat piles parallel to the rows, and the seed heads were stacked into little mounds nearby. When the entire cane patch had been cut, the wagons came through and hauled the cane to the mill to be made into sorghum molasses.

Later, the grain heads were hauled to the barn, threaded onto long wires and hung in the rafters to dry—away from the mice. There they'd remain until some winter afternoon when Papa would take them down, pound them between two boards to release the seeds, bag the winnowed seeds and hang them in the rafters to await the next planting season.

We children always felt sorry for the horses that had to go around (and around and around) so many times to grind the juice from the cane at the mill; but it was such fun to see the green juice pour down the little chute into the barrel below. The piles of "pummies" grew higher and higher as the crushed cane came through the mill.

School almost always had started by the time molasses cooking began, and we children seldom got to see the entire cooking process; but we always tried to get in on the best part of it. As soon as the bell rang to dismiss school, we would grab our books and lunch buckets and head for home on the run.

After a quick stop at the house, we would make for the sorghum mill and usually arrive just as the molasses was being emptied from the big pan into the ten-gallon lard cans. Then Papa would pass out the little wooden paddles he had whittled and the feast began! Nothing ever tasted better than the freshly made sorghum molasses that stuck to the bottom and sides of the big pan.

The heavy cans of warm sorghum molasses then were loaded onto the wagon and hauled to the house where they were stored in the pantry. There they remained, ready to be opened on some winter evening when Mama got out her favorite recipes that called for sorghum molasses. Papa didn't need a recipe for his specialty, which he called "Lick-dab." He poured a generous serving of sorghum molasses onto his plate from the molasses pitcher on the table, then blended in just the right amount of soft butter to make his favorite spread.

Mama, however, had a 100-year old recipe for soft gingerbread. She would grease and flour the big baking pan which measured about 8 by 15-inches. Then she would preheat the oven to 350° before she started whipping up the gingerbread batter in the large crock.

While she measured the other ingredients, she'd let my sister and me cream the ½ cup of lard with 1 cup of sugar. Sometimes we'd take a taste or two, but she scolded us because she said it would spoil the proportions in the recipe.

Two beaten eggs and 1 cup of molasses went into the batter next. Last of all, Mama would alternate 1 cup of buttermilk with a mixture of 3 cups of flour, 2 teaspoons baking soda, 2 teaspoons each of ginger, cinnamon and allspice and ½ teaspoon each of cloves and nutmeg.

After Mama emptied the gingerbread into the baking pan, we got to scrape the mixing bowl. When we could smell the gingerbread baking, Mama would open the oven carefully and thrust a broom straw into the middle of the loaf. If it came out clean, she knew the gingerbread was done.

Another family favorite was "Popcorn Brittle." And although the recipe was lost for many years, I found a copy of it this past summer—scrawled in childish handwriting on a brown paper wrapper among some old recipes which my mother had clipped.

This is how we made it: Boil 3 cups brown sugar, 1 cup of molasses and ½ teaspoon cream of tartar in a large kettle until a little syrup forms a hard ball when dropped into cold water.

Melt ½ cup butter and mix it with the syrup. Then, when it's well-blended, add 1 quart of popped corn and stir. Remove from the stove and add 2 teaspoons of soda, dissolved in 2 tablespoons of hot water.

Stir briskly and when the mixture froths, turn it out onto a buttered platter. Spread it thinly and evenly. When it's cool, break it into small pieces.

(But, be sure the kettle is large enough, for this candy increases in volume—almost magically!)

Molasses-making time brings such pleasant memories to mind that I've decided I'm going to get some freshly-made sorghum molasses this fall and try these old recipes which Mama made when we were children. In all these years, I've never tasted anything which compares to the delight of Mama's molasses goodies.

Ruth Straight Hibbs

Autumn Fanfare

When dreamy hills are veiled with hazy mist
In mellow shades of golden amethyst;
And purple grapes are clustered overhead
While stately sumacs flaunt their plumes of red,
The squirrels frolic where the chestnuts fall;
Where katydids and saucy bluejays call,
From cornfields where the golden pumpkins lie,
And arrowed geese are etched against the sky—
The winds, in jolly fanfare, greet the leaves,
And mingle rainbow colors in the breeze.

Caroline Henning Bair

When autumn blends her colors
In a panoramic view
Over fields, woods, and hillsides
In variegated hue,
We stand and gaze in wonder
At the lavishness arrayed
In the beauty and the vastness
Of God's handiwork displayed.

Ottis Shirk

Grandparents' Day
A Time for Gratitude

For everything you are and everything you have, you owe a debt to those who came before and who will not pass this way again. Via Presidential Proclamation dated August 3, 1978, National Grandparents' Day came into being. Marian McQuade of West Virginia, mother of fifteen children, and Mike Goldgar, a Georgia man inspired by the birth of his first grandchild, are co-founders of this special American day of tribute to grandparents. Both attribute their keen interest in establishing the event to the pervasive loneliness they observed when visiting relatives in nursing homes. Whatever the reason, Grandparents' Day is overdue, welcome, and warranted!

President Carter, in establishing the first Sunday after Labor Day as Grandparents' Day, stated:

"Each American family is similarly shaped and guided by its forebears. Just as a nation learns and is strengthened by its history, so a family learns and is strengthened by its understanding of preceding generations. As Americans live longer, more and more families are enriched by their shared experiences with grandparents and great-grandparents.

"The elders of each family have the responsibility for setting the moral tone for the family and for passing on the traditional values of our nation to their children and grandchildren. They bore the hardships and made the sacrifices that produced much of the progress and comfort we enjoy today. It is appropriate, therefore, that as individuals and as a nation, that we salute our grandparents for their contribution to our lives."

The concept that a special day be set aside to honor those helpful, unassuming, seldom-demanding senior citizens responsible for the rest of us being on the face of this earth has been a long time in coming. But Grandparents' Day, now just a year old, sets one thinking and posing questions to which there may not be satisfactory answers. Why is it that "loneliness" and "aloneness" seem destined to be the constant companions of people whose only "fault" has been an accumulation of years? Why is it, after a lifetime of experience and learning which produced a rich lode of empirical knowledge, hardly anyone listens to what grandparents have to say? While the "race may go to the swift," since when did we begin equating speed and endurance with intelligence and dignity? Why isn't every day in the year Grandparents' Day? It ought to be!

Gale Brennan

WONDERS OF NATURE

The Old Hometown

I want to go back to the old hometown,
   To a little white house all trimmed in brown;
To walk down the road where redbud sway,
   And sit neath the oaks where I used to play.

I want to see folks whom I used to know;
   I want to go places where I used to go.
I want to go down to the big dripping spring
   And sit on the moss where I used to sing.

I want to go back to the little church house,
   Where I used to go in my starched-up blouse,
Where the preacher would smile and kindly say:
   "My boy, I am glad you came today."

I want to go back to the old hometown,
   To a little white house all trimmed in brown,
To walk down the road where redbud sway
   And sit neath the oaks where I used to play.

Cecil Brown

AUTUMN AND THE FIVE SENSES

Maxine McCray Miller

AUTUMN

IS A TIME FOR SEEING

the glory of living color; the red and gold of hills and dales; the multicolored corn peeping from the shock; the orange of fine pumpkins; the delicate white lace of frost traced on the window-panes; brown pinecones nestled in the green of pines; scarlet bittersweet berries; purple grapes; the gold of a harvest moon and jack-o'-lanterns with amber lights. It is a time for seeing witches, goblins, ghosts, and skipping gnomes, and Mother making jam and jelly.

AUTUMN

IS A TIME FOR HEARING

wind that drums a tune on roof-tops; the whirring wings of star-tled quail; the chatter of squir-rels hiding nuts away; school bells, school buses and school lessons. It is a time for hearing the crackle of hay as kittens cuddle down in nests for warmth; the turn of grinders making ap-ple cider; the fiddle playing at the harvest dance; the call of highways leading to fall pano-ramas and happy songs ringing around campfires.

AUTUMN

IS A TIME FOR TASTING

tantalizing pumpkin and mince pies; rich, crunchy nuts; boxed school lunches, fall banquets and lamplit family dinners. It is a time for tasting trick-or-treat candy, Thanksgiving turkey and new recipes gathered from the girls at the church supper.

AUTUMN
IS A TIME FOR SMELLING

the smoke of Indian summer and burning leaves; the fragrance of chrysanthemums; the pungent pine in fireplaces; the musky odor of foliage in damp woodlands; the spicy air of kitchens; sweet clover in haylofts and that strange, illusive aroma that tells the person close to nature that the first snow is on the way.

AUTUMN
IS A TIME FOR TOUCHING

dreams of hand and heart and gathering their reality; the ripened grain; the gratified shining vision; the luscious peach and apple . . . hope for tomorrow; the realization of the goodness of friends, family, and God. It is a time for touching the coins of labor and love and the edge of infinity . . . the time we come to know in grateful hearts that in this hour of reaping we have again harvested golden fruits of a living faith and its abundant fulfillment.

Autumnfest

Nature holds a festival,
The highlight of the year.
It's autumn's colorama,
When all the trees appear.

Dressed in their brightest garments
And standing on display,
Just waiting to be noticed
By all who come their way.

She's full of glad surprises;
She's rich with gems and gold.
Come, fill your heart and pockets
With all that they can hold.

She spreads a crimson carpet
For you to walk upon.
Her waving branches beckon:
"Come out and join the fun!"

She showers you with confetti,
As leaves come drifting down;
Her gay mood is contagious,
As festive as her gown.

Frances Huisman

Autumn Splendor

Who looks upon an autumn tree,
Aflame in scarlet or in gold,
Will stand in breathless wonderment
And feed his soul a thousandfold.

Who looks upon an autumn hill
Will there behold the Artist's hand
That wrought in splendor overnight
A glowing jeweled wonderland.

Who feasts on autumn's loveliness
Retains the memory of it long;
And it will lift his spirit up,
And warm him like a treasured song.

Who looks upon a world ablaze
With color, starred with goldenrod,
Will know that he is privileged
To see the masterpiece of God.

William Arnette Wofford

Indian summer holds the landscape,
Warm and tender its embrace;
Brilliant hues and somber shadings
Side by side and interlace.

Softest green has turned to scarlet,
Glowing bronze and brightest gold;
Riotous color spreads its beauty,
Vibrant, gay, and bold.

Trees all dressed in gayest foliage
Whirl and dance on autumn days,
O'er the hills and o'er the lowlands
Lies a misty, smoky haze.

Warm and golden sunshine filters
Low to ripen harvest wheat,
Pumpkins glow beside the doorstep,
Mellow in the autumn heat.

Smoke swirls drift across the landscape,
Pungent its familiar scent,
Busy days and days of pleasure,
Ere the autumn days are spent.

Autumn days and Indian summer,
Wild and free as gypsy band,
O to wander and to revel,
When Indian summer holds the land.

Naomi I. Parks

Early in the morning
There is frost upon the ground;
And in many other places
It can easily be found,
Till the sunshine from a cloudless sky,
Which reaches far and near,
Soon by the warmth of its magic touch
Makes the cold frost disappear.

A clear day, moderate-warm, and mild,
But a long and distant gaze
Reveals along the horizon
A misty, smoky haze.
In the atmosphere the smell of smoke
Comes floating on the air,
And the rustle of autumn's fallen leaves
Is heard under trees now bare.

The wild geese are winging southward,
Wedge-shaped against the sky,
And the summer birds with their chirps and songs,
Have said their long good-bye.
With this sudden change of season,
Birds still seek their southern clime,
There's a Power that seems to tell them,
"It's only Indian summertime."

Ottis Shirk

A Moment of Beauty

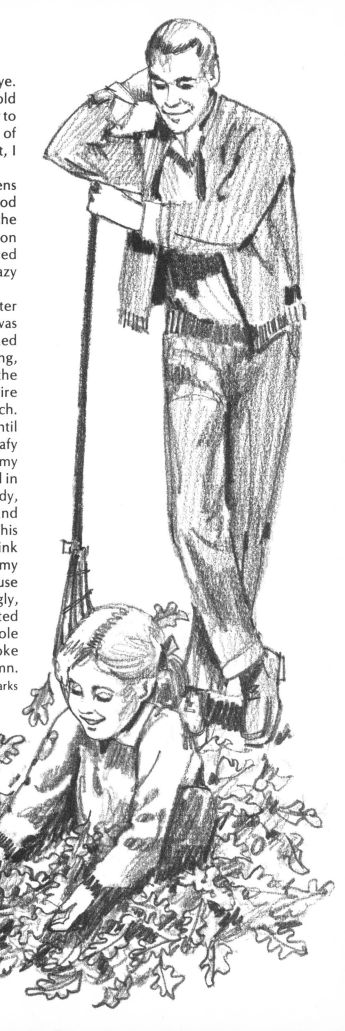

Glancing out my window, a flash of color catches my eye. Dancing on the fingers of the wind, its brilliant red-gold glinting with the sun's reflections, a maple leaf drifts slowly to the ground to be lost in anonymity among the myriad of leaves already fallen. Sensing the beauty of this moment, I remember another autumn.

The pageant of the setting sun had painted the heavens in a spectrum of vivid hues rivaled only by the trees that stood beneath its canopy. The air was crisp and cool, tinged with the acrid smell of smoke. The trees, garbed in a motley of crimson and golds, dropped their cover and the falling leaves faltered through the motionless air to blanket the ground in a crazy quilt of riotous color.

It was early evening, and I remember dashing out after supper, bundled against the coming chill. The rake was propped against the house, a reminder of my chore. I picked it up and scuffled lazily into the yard, every crackling, crunching step filling me with delight. Standing alone in the profusion of leaves, I began to rake. Each stroke, with the wire tines scraping the hard ground beneath, cleared a little patch. I worked tirelessly and contentedly, pushing and piling, until at last the yard was clean and bare—stripped of its leafy blanket. But before me—heaped high and inviting—lay my leaves. Without hesitation, I took a flying leap and landed in the center of the pile, letting the leaves cover my body, reveling at their crack and rustle to my every movement, and breathing the sweetish smell of their beginning decay. This was peace. Buoyed on their cushion, I could dream and think alone—hidden by nature from the world. I continued in my reverie until, at twilight, my father emerged from the house and called me from the pile. Then, quickly and unfeelingly, he set a match to it. As I watched—the first leaf ignited quickly, and the tongues of flame soon infected the whole pile. Before long my beautiful mound was reduced to smoke and black ash. Such a waste of beauty. But this was autumn.

Sharon Sparks

A Day of Reflections

This is a day of reflections,
Reflections of summer past;
A look to the distant hillsides
And down through the valleys vast

Brings panoramas of beauty;
The trees tinged with rust and gold
Spell autumn in big bold letters;
How much of splendor they hold!

I see the cornfields stand mutely,
All shocked and rustling with wind;
I see the pumpkins there sitting
(And not in the least chagrined).

Yes, this is a day for reflections;
I think of the summer past.
But, oh, the beauties of autumn . . .
Their grandeur is unsurpassed!

Georgia B. Adams

Autumn's Yield

Have ever bluer skies or mirrored depths of streams
Stirred the heart more with soul-enriching dreams?
Fulfillment and serenity now wander hand in hand
To cast a warming glow upon quiescent land.
Blue haze on distant hills beckons enticingly
Stirring gypsy blood to newborn ecstasy.
What a privilege it is to share in nature's gold
That memory can store and ever after hold
In measure, brimming over with spirit-warming yields
Found in the vibrant beauty of frost-kissed autumn fields.

Johanna Ter Wee

Victorian Glass

H. Russell Zimmermann

"Stained glass" has become the catchall term to describe almost everything produced during the Victorian art glass boom. Many of the pieces, which are now conveniently called stained-glass windows, do not actually belong to that group. During the last half of the nineteenth century, when the fad for ornamental windows reached its peak, there were no less than three-dozen words to describe the variety of products available. The nation had become so infected by this rage that by 1880, there were nearly 24,000 craftsmen in the business of creating "fancy glass" for everything from saloon windows to umbrella stands. In nearly all cases the finished article was a combination of two or more of the basic techniques then popular.

Ornamental windows in the home may seem to be a logical outgrowth of the mainstream of Victorian taste, but they had, in fact, a slow start and were accepted with great difficulty. As late as the 1870s H. Hudson Holly wrote, "Many think that stained glass gives a house too much the appearance of a church. . . . Stained glass in our houses seems such an innovation that the majority of people, taking custom only as their guide, are astonished at the mere suggestion." Overcoming the ecclesiastical connotation was such a problem for architects, that, in the early years, some were forced to use the colored light fad as an excuse to include an ornamental glass window in the plan. (At that time—1860s & 70s—it was believed that light rays of certain colors were good for the health and could even cure ailments.)

But when the stigma was removed, the country took off on a glass binge which had no equal in the long history of the craft. Criticism of this unrestrained spree began in the nineteenth century and has never ceased. It has been called the "decline," "deplorable," and "the final degradation of the stained-glass window." True, there are uncounted thousands of tasteless, bizarre, and sometimes just plain ugly windows still to be seen throughout the country, but there were also a number of notable and worthwhile contributors during the same period. Freed from technical restrictions by the industrial revolution, Victorian craftsmen created new techniques and materials which gave vitality and character to glass not exhibited before.

From top to bottom: Bevel Ground Plate Glass Prisms, Rolled Cathedral Glass, Roundel Window, French Embossed Glass, Ground Flashed Glass.

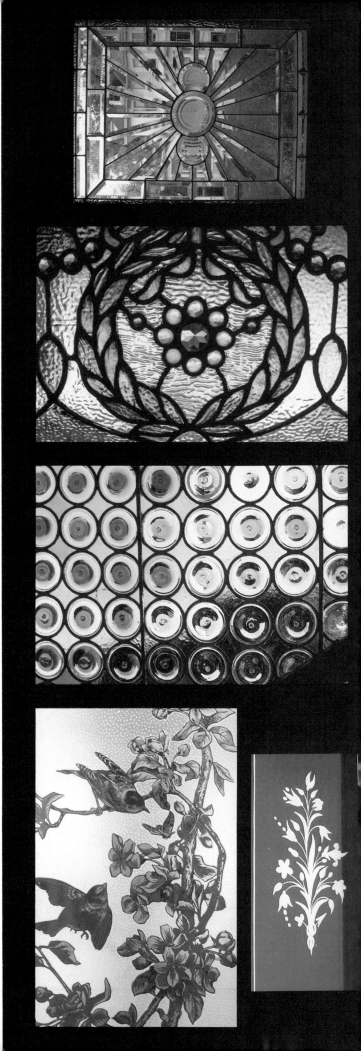

The following are descriptions of the types of glass, new and old, which were available to the nineteenth century craftsman, the surface treatments used on them, as well as the various techniques of construction, and special added materials.

Types of Glass

Cathedral glass (also called "rolled cathedral," "Hartley's rolled," or "figure-rolled"). This is a rolled glass produced mechanically by "casting" or pouring the molten glass on a table and rolling it out like pie dough. One surface was usually imprinted with a texture, either by the table or the roller. This process was developed and patented by James Hartley in 1847. Edward Armitage, a prominent English stained-glass artist, wrote "To any one, except the expert, cathedral glass suggests the highest grade of material reserved more especially for our finest cathedrals, whereas it is in fact the lowest type of glass which should never adorn anything higher than, let us say, a domestic bathroom." Its principal shortcoming is the monotonous effect produced by the mechanical texture.

Antique glass (also called "pot metal" and "colored cylinder glass"). A hand blown glass produced to imitate the beautiful character of that produced during the Middle Ages. The artisan would gather a gob of glass on the end of his blowpipe and gently blow a spherical bubble. With reheating and swinging of the pipe to create centrifugal force, the bubble was finally extended into a cylinder called the "muff." The ends were cut off and the muff was scored and cracked along its length. When placed in the flattening kiln, score-side up, the cylinder would slowly open and fall into a flat rectangular sheet. The beauty of the sheet was in the small bubbles, imperfections, and variations in color caused by uneven thickness.

Streaky glass A variation of antique glass in which the blowpipe is dipped into various pots and worked into one mass before blowing. The effect produced was a wavy, marbleized wafting of two or more colors.

Flashed glass (also called cased glass). A thin layer of colored glass on the surface of a sheet of clear antique glass. In this variation the blower would gather his clear gob and then dip it in the colored melt before blowing the cylinder. It was a method of backing up certain glasses having such intense color (i.e. cobalt blue, gold ruby) as to be almost opaque if made the usual 1/8-inch thick. The thinness of the flashed layer renders the color more compatible with others and offers the possibility of etching.

From top to bottom: Tiffany Glass and Construction, Ground Sandblast Glass, True Example of Silver Staining, Zinc Came Construction, Etched Glass.

Bottle glass (also called "slab glass," "Norman slab," or "English Norman slab"). In this process a glassblower begins a bubble, lowers it into a rectangular box, and then blows until the box is filled, forming a square bottle with a domed top. When cool the flat sides and the bottom are cut out yielding 5 slabs thick in the center and thin at the edges. Slabs are used where more prism-like refraction of light is desired.

Opal glass (also called "milky" or "opalescent"). An infinite variety of opal glasses were developed ranging from a faint milkiness to complete opacity. The effect of cloud or milkiness is due to microscopic particles of one clear glass imbedded in another clear glass of a different refractive index. Opals were often used in conjunction with transparents to form patterns which were visible even when there was no light passing through the window.

Surface Treatments

Staining In the fourteenth century it was discovered that by applying silver nitrate to glass and firing it in a kiln, a yellow stain was produced. The resulting golden color was more brilliant and beautiful than a pot metal glass, which was colored in the solid. The staining of glass was always done on the back, and was used to make designs by itself, back up a painted drawing, or change the color of a piece of glass (i.e., blue glass stained with yellow would make a vibrant green).

Painting As the name implies, painting was simply the application of hand-painted design to the pieces of glass. The pigment used was finely powdered fusible glass mixed with metallic oxides which produced color when the finished piece was fired in the kiln. Simple black line drawings, pinstriping, and flat patterns could be accomplished in one firing. When a richly colored landscape, portrait, or still life was required, the craftsman had to make many trips to the kiln. With each subsequent firing there would be the need to strengthen a line, deepen a color, or make additional corrections. The finished painting was fused to the glass and would therefore withstand the weather virtually forever. (There are many windows in Europe dating back to the eleventh century in which the painting is still well preserved.)

Etching (also known as "embossing"). Hydroflouric acid was discovered by a Swedish chemist (Scheele) in the eighteenth century and was found to readily dissolve glass. The Victorians jumped at the chance to use this principle for the ornamentation of plate glass and applied it to everything from textured opaque bathroom windows to delicate floral designs which became focal points of the house. Original pencil designs were placed under the glass and traced over with a brush and a resist of "Brunswick black" or "Japan" black. A ½-inch high dam was then flooded with acid. Acid ate into the glass where it was not painted; the longer it remained on the surface

the deeper the etching. When the acid and the resist were washed off, a two level design was left. One later variation was "stippling," in which a thin layer of gum Arabic and mica chips were sifted over the plate before etching. These loose particles caused uneven biting and resulted in an unusual textured surface. One of the most important uses of acid was to cut through the thin colored layer of flashed glass to reveal a design in white (i.e. in a heraldic shield a Latin motto might be etched in white through blue flashed glass).

French embossing(also known as "triple embossing"). One of the most beautiful and delicate techniques to come out of nineteenth century work. In principle it was etching flashed glass, but with a great deal more intricacy. The artist would hand paint a design in resist and give it an acid bath. After washing, more embossing varnish was applied followed by still another etch. Many times under the acid and very careful planning created a piece in which there might be three levels of clear glass and three levels of colored flash. (This would yield two pinks and a deep ruby from one thin layer of red.) It is obvious that this technique was time-consuming and costly. As a result, these windows are rare and valuable.

Sandblasting (also "art sandblasting glass" or frosted glass). Like etching, sandblasting produced a fine translucent texture on the surface of a sheet and was most often used to create ornamental inserts in front doors. In 1870, a Philadelphia chemist Benjamin Tilghman, patented a revolutionary system which used high-pressure steam, air, or water to propel a stream of sand. Fine white sand was used for delicate work, while crushed flint would make deeper cuts. Designs were made by masking the plate glass before blasting. There were numerous masks or stencils including rubber, rubber coated zinc, thin mild steel sheet, and parchment paper protected by an elastic varnish. The mask had to be resilient enough to make the sand bounce off instead of cut in.

Chipped glass (also "frost pattern"). This amazing process began with a sheet of glass which had been evenly sandblasted. It was then coated with a special glue and subjected to gradual heating. As the glue dried it would shrink with tremendous force and flake off the sheet. Each flake caused a chip of glass to break away from the surface. The result was a brilliant and shiny fractured glass texture that resembled large frost crystals. "Double chipping" was simply a second application of the same. Chipped glass was used for glass signs with gold leaf and in prism windows.

Engraved glass A small revolving copper wheel at the end of a long spindle was fed with oil and emery powder. The glass was worked against the wheel and ground away. On flashed glass beautiful designs were cut through the colored layer to reveal white. On clear or sandblasted glass an engraved design was polished until it resembled fine crystal stemware.

Prism glass (also "cut glass," "brilliant cut," "bevel plate," "faceted glass"). Beveling, or the grinding of angled surfaces, was done on a sandstone wheel or an iron wheel using an abrasive and water. Thick pieces of glass were first cut into decorative shapes and then beveled on all sides. Smoothing was done on willow wood or cork wheels with pumice and water. Finally the pieces were polished with a revolving fiber brush and rouge until they looked like the prisms of a crystal chandelier. They were used in colored glass windows as accents or leaded together to form whole windows of bevel glass. When sunlight streams through one of these windows it is refracted into thousands of colored rainbows.

Pressed glass (also "jewels" and "cutstones"). Many Victorian windows had faceted gem-like accents in clear or colored glass. These "jewels" were pressed in iron molds while the glass was hot. In rare cases they were as large as 4-inches in diameter and had ground and polished facets.

Bullseyes (also "rondels" or "roundels"). These familiar circular pieces were used as accents or leaded together in imitation of the late medieval secular windows. The best were handblown and showed the fracture where the glass blower's "punty" was broken off. Others were pressed to simulate the genuine article.

Tiffany glass Louis C. Tiffany devoted the greater portion of his life to experimenting with glass. He contributed a number of techniques which gave richness and refinement to art glass windows at the end of the century. His famous iridescence was made by exposing the surface of glass to metallic oxides and chemical vapors. He produced another type of glass by scattering filaments of colored glass over clear sheets and rolling them together. Perhaps his most creative contribution was the use of corrugating rollers and "roughened tools" to create a heavily textured glass. With these carefully selected pieces he was able to simulate three-dimensional drapery folds and foliage which not only looked good as transparencies, but had great richness at night when the window was illuminated from the inside.

Construction Techniques

Leading The use of "H" shaped lead strips, called cames, is as old as the Christian art of stained glass. In the nineteenth century it was by far the most common method of construction. After cutting, all of the small glass pieces were held in place by fitting them edge-to-edge into both sides of the "H." At each intersection of cames soldering on both sides of the window held the joint together. The window was finished by scrubbing a putty-like cement into the spaces between the lead lip and the glass. This weather-sealed and tightened the final product.

Rigid came Near the end of the century zinc and copper cames were introduced as alternates to leading. Although basically the same as leading, the new cames were more rigid and used in the assembly of prism windows and clear glass sash with straight lines (i.e. diamond panes).

Tiffany The most tedious and time-consuming construction was Tiffany's. Each piece of glass was edged with a glued-on strip of copper foil which slightly overlapped both faces. When all pieces were bordered this way and pressed into their final positions edge-to-edge, solder was applied to the gaps. By flowing between the pieces, and pooling on top and bottom, a solder shape similar to the "H" lead came was formed. The beauty of this technique was the quality of black line it made when rear-illuminated. It had an interesting variable width, but it was also the thinnest line possible with any techinque.

Mosaic A spectacular effect was obtained by using tiny square and triangular pieces of glass set up in metallic grout. It was almost identical to a mosaic, but being exposed on both sides instead of one, it was transparent.

The foregoing materials and processes are the more common and obvious ones. There were many more which represented one craftsman's individual experimentation or an unpopular short-lived technique. Windows exhibiting a single style of construction or material can be found, but in most cases two or more were used on the same job. It is not uncommon to find very complicated windows such as a leaded art glass window with a painted vignette, bevel plate prisms, pressed jewels, and etched flashed glass.

By the turn of the century even millwork catalogs had large sections in color showing standard window designs available from twenty-two cents per square foot (single process chipped glass) to $4.00 per square foot for leaded bevel plate. The best windows were not from catalogs, but were one-of-a-kind commissions custom-made to fit the character and size of a given room setting.

The United States seems to be experiencing a rediscovery of stained glass, but it may never again show the fervor and creativity of the Victorian boom. And to fully appreciate our nineteenth century art glass, it should be viewed from the proper perspective, as suggested in this statement from an 1880 issue of "The Builder": "Whether high or low in scale of color, a stained glass window is essentially decorative art, and the more decorative, we might say . . . the more sumptuous it is, the better it fulfills its purpose as a part of the whole."

Autumn Told Me

I wandered up a long hill path
That climbed toward flaming sunset skies;
Where wild grape tangles tinged the air
With musty sweetness; there arise
The yellow aspen and scrub oak,
Hovering small life with meager shade;
While rifting through the taller pines
Thin shafts of slanting sunlight played.
Softly the haze of harvest air
Prophesied the winter's sleep;
Flaming sumac and goldenrod
Vied with the color of bittersweet,
As if to hoard that which summer lost
To the grasping fingers of early frost.

Grace R. Ballard

Come Share with Me

Come sing with me the mountains' song:
Blue air through aspen trees,
And water washing age-old stones—
Come be a part of these.

Come watch with me the width of sky,
That velvet depthless blue;
Come see the sun paint lemon flame
Across the hills for you.

Come share with me this timeless land,
The dawn, the tumbling stream;
Come hear the wind's long-whispered tales,
And keep a song to dream.

Virginia Covey Boswell

A Love of Beauty

I believe that love of beauty is born in us all to some degree. I can't help but believe this is true, for everything in Nature is beautiful. Nature has long been a life study by many, and the entire world bows in appreciation. No matter where one goes on this globe, there he will find beauty sufficient to satisfy the hungriest lover of what this world has to offer.

Nature is full of miraculous designs that man has copied over and over again. My home grounds are a riot of color now. Art and beauty of every description. I now fill my hands with leaves and am left in a state of wonder. How did these autumn leaves get their magnificent color? Hold a fallen maple leaf to the light and note what a perfect piece of art and beauty it is. The circulation of life to the minutest corner of these leaves should be sufficient to fortify the faith of us all.

God's trees had to be supported by these leaves, which give them life, and we easily remain in a state of wonder whenever we touch anything that grows, or moves, in Nature. A child is quick to make a mental note of color, even though we know we are ignorant of the thoughts that romp in a child's brain. How sensitive each one of us is toward all beauty, and all creation, anyway!

Many of the tiniest flowers, that grow in hidden places, rarely known but by experts, when put under a microscope, reveal an art design that is unbelievable. It also calls our attention to the fact that God created everywhere!

George Matthew Adams

Twice Blessed

At mountaintop where land touches sky,
   Contentment holds the passerby,
And thoughts that hills, wildlife, and man
   Are each a part of God's great plan.

From rocky crest where eagles sail,
   Strong hearts look down the treelined trail
Beyond the lake, an icy cup,
   Where timid deer and wild bear sup,

To see the hills become a ridge . . .
   A fallen tree has formed a bridge.
Some unseen hand, this beauty spills
   And tucks the valley round the hills.

While far below the road unwinds
   Past patchwork fields and clustered vines,
Through orchards hanging full and grand,
   A ribbon through the harvest land.

The hills hold beauty in their hands.
   The bear in shining splendor stands.
All share God's gifts in many ways,
   But only man can sing His praise.

Sara Bren

© Walter Lantz

Woody 1945

Walter and Woody

Woody 1941

Andy Panda, Chilly Willy, Gabby Gator, and Col. Heeza Liar are part of the world created by cartoonist Walter Lantz. It is, however, the incomparable Woody Woodpecker for which Lantz is most well-known and most closely identified.

In his fifty-eight year career, Walter Lantz has experienced many changes. He began his career drawing newspaper comic strip characters for Morrell Goddard (The Katzenjammer Kids, Happy Hooligan, and Krazy Kat), then went to work at the newly opened cartoon studio of Gregory LaCava where Lantz created and directed "Pete the Pup" and "Dinky Doodle." In 1922 he produced his first cartoon series, "Col. Heeza Liar," which became one of the most famous of silent cartoons.

In 1926, Lantz moved from New York to Universal Studios in Hollywood as a film producer where he enjoyed the longest producer-studio relationship in show business. His first project was the Oswald Rabbit cartoons which he produced for ten years. Lantz then spearheaded the first Technicolor cartoon, "The King of Jazz," featuring the Paul Whiteman orchestra and the Rhythm Boys trio (of which Bing Crosby was a member).

In 1941, two important events took place in Lantz's life. First, he married Broadway and screen actress Grace Stafford. Second, on their honeymoon on Sherwood Lake in the Santa Monica mountains, the roof of the cottage was pecked through by a very persistent little woodpecker. From this event, the idea of the irascible Woody Woodpecker was born. Lantz began drawing Woody into his Andy Panda cartoons, and Woody gained such acceptance he was soon into mischief of his own.

In an effort to find a distinctive voice and laugh for the wacky woodpecker, Lantz listened to hundreds of recordings by well-known voice experts. He selected one, the recording artist unknown to him. The voice belonged to Mrs. Lantz who continues to provide the voice and crazy laugh of Woody Woodpecker.

Since cartoon production costs have skyrocketed, Lantz has changed his medium one more time; he now paints scenic landscapes in which he incorporates his cartoon characters and has coined the name "happy art." Lantz mainly uses the High Sierras for subject matter, in which he and Grace have a summer home. He studied seriously with the famed landscape artist Robert Wood to perfect his technique. His "happy art" has been a huge success, grossing over $300,000 in 1978.

Lantz has been recognized and honored many times by those in the field of animation. In 1972, he was the guest of honor at the Animated Film Festival in Zagreb, Yugoslavia. In 1973, he received the Annie Award, "the Oscar of animation," from the Association Internationale du Film d'Animation. And in 1978, his films were shown at the Museum of Modern Art in New York City and at the Filmex '78 in Los Angeles. In addition, earlier this year, the Motion Picture Academy of Arts and Sciences presented an honorary Oscar to Woody's creator.

Woody 1960

A model for all people with a zest for living, the Lantzes encourage laughter and happiness. Their own personal cheer and that brought about through Woody and the other cartoon characters are spread world-wide. Who can help but laugh along with Woody? "Ha, ha, ha, HA, ha. Ha, ha, HA, ha, ha. Huhuhuhuhuhuhu!"

Shari Style

Woody 1950

Autumn Encounter

D. Stuart Briscoe

The few frantic weeks of the summer season had crowded the lakeside with people from the cities. They had arrived in their brightly colored busses, which were parked end-to-end round the gentle contours of Bowness Bay, all but obliterating the view of water, choppy in the stiff summer breezes. The local people, knowing their annual income depended on the brief invasion of tourists, swallowed hard as the excited screams of the young people punctuated the blare of their music and ripped the silence of the lakes to shreds. They pretended not to notice the football games that sprang up on the flower-bordered lawns as the tourists tired of looking at the view and throwing stones in the water. When evening came and the crowds departed the "locals" cleaned up the mess, banked their takings and braced themselves for tomorrow.

But today was different because summer and her attendant crowds had departed and autumn had arrived. Gone were the sudden summer squalls which kicked up spume on the lake and sent the boats scurrying for shelter. The skies were cleared of the majestic cumulus clouds which added depth to the landscape, but insistently robbed persistent sunbathers of what little tan they hoped to eke out of the fitful sun. The boats had been stored for winter, the lawns resodded, and the flower beds emptied of flowers and prepared for the therapy of winter's harsh massage.

As I walked around the bay which lies about half way along the eastern shore of Lake Windermere, England's largest lake, I noticed that the first snows had fallen on the mountains around Ambleside. For most of the summer those same mountains had been hidden from view either by low clouds or summer haze, but on this occasion they stood clearly edged against an uncommonly blue English sky. There was no trace of breeze and the sun was pleasantly warm despite the definite frosty edge which autumn had brought with her. Sitting on a solitary seat I looked across to Belle Isle in the centre of the lake remembering the stories my father told of the bitter winters of his youth when horses had pulled carts loaded with coal across the ice. I smiled to myself as I looked at the place where he had fallen into the lake because he had been so engrossed in the small boat he was pulling that he had overlooked the fact that he was running out of pier.

Without me realizing it, autumn had got to me and I was in a most unaccustomed melancholy mood. Perhaps the brilliant, blazing banks of multicolored leaves, duplicated so sharply in the lake water that I could not tell where reflections started and originals ended, had directed me on a reflective train of thought. I was soon interrupted by a scampering squirrel heading unerringly up the gnarled trunk of an old beech tree. I watched her as she hopped and leaped, picking up acorns and beechnuts, and rushed as if her very life depended upon it to her precarious pantry in the branches above. Of course, her very life did depend upon her preparations, as did the life of the geese which suddenly came into view, flying by some incalculable instinct from the imminent, northern winter to more congenial climate and circumstances. Long necks stretched, powerful wings beating clear air in slow rhythmic strokes, they headed south in V formation which reminded me of the World War II bombers I had seen in my youth roaring into the night on missions of devastation.

Impatient with my thoughts, I jumped up from the seat and started back towards the office where my work was waiting in neat piles for the conclusion of my lunch break. Why had autumn done this to me? Surely autumn was the time to rejoice in the tranquillity, thrill to the blazing colors, and drink in the crispness that only a touch of frost can bring. To reinforce my own conclusions, I reached down and scooped up an armful of leaves from the tree-lined path. They were indescribably beautiful and, to my dismay, indisputably dead!

Autumn speaks in tones as muted as her colors are glorious. She whispers thoughts of warm days, of opportunity gone by, and adds gentle reminders of chilling days of consequence to come. Her message came early to the prematurely-aged Lord Byron as he wrote,

> "My days are in the yellow leaf;
> The flowers and fruits of love are gone;
> The worm, the canker, and the grief
> Are mine alone!"

Yet he had understood only half her message. Where was the heeding of the geese and the reading of the squirrel's lesson? Standing in striking contrast to the blazing colors of the dying leaves a row of tall pines added their richness to the scene. Green, the most restful of all colors, was their distinctive. Not for them the brilliant explosion of autumn shades leading to stark nakedness through long winter months. Just simple, deep quiet green of the greatest kind: evergreen.

The sight of them lent a paradoxical spring to my step. They reminded me of commitments of years gone by to be the kind of man whose "delight is in the law of the Lord, and on his law he meditates day and night." For I knew that then, and only then, through God's grace, I would be,

> "Like a tree planted by the streams of water,
> which yields its fruit in season
> and whose leaf does not wither."

Chrysanthemums

It blooms in splendor, bursting forth
   Along the garden row . . .
I've even seen this stalwart soul
   Outlive an early snow.

It lifts its heavy flowered head
   With bold and haughty sweep,
Unmindful that the other plants
   Are going off to sleep.

The bouquets of mums I gather
   Stay fresh and bright for days;
They bring a sparkle to the house
   That nothing else conveys.

When summer days have ended and
   A chill does nip the air,
I love the bright chrysanthemum
   With all its beauty rare.

I'm sure God sends chrysanthemums
   To cheer us in the fall,
To help us gather strength and hope
   Ere winter comes to call.

Peggy Mlcuch

The Columbian Oration

This day belongs not to America, but to the world. The results of the event it commemorates are the heritage of the peoples of every race and clime. We celebrate the emancipation of man. The preparation was the work of almost countless centuries; the realization was the revelation of one. The Cross on Calvary was hope; the cross raised on San Salvador was opportunity. But for the first, Columbus would never have sailed; but for the second, there would have been no place for the planting, the nurture, and the expansion of civil and religious liberty.

The spirit of Columbus hovers over us today. Only by celestial intelligence can it grasp the full significance of this spectacle and ceremonial.

From the first century to the fifteenth counts for little in the history of progress, but in the period between the fifteenth and twentieth is crowded the romance and reality of human development. Life has been prolonged, and its enjoyment intensified. The powers of the air and the water, the resistless forces of the elements, which in the time of the discoverer were the visible terrors of the wrath of God, have been subdued to the service of man. Arts and luxuries which could be possessed and enjoyed only by the rich and noble, the works of genius which were read and understood only by the learned few, domestic comforts and surroundings beyond the reach of lord or bishop, now adorn and illumine the homes of our citizens.

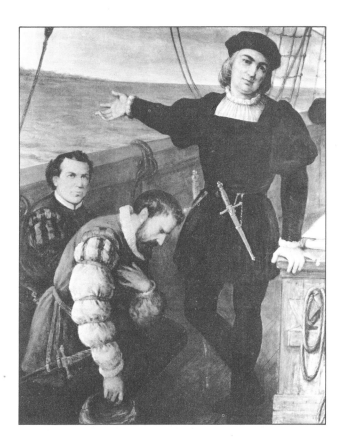

Serfs are sovereigns and the people are kings. The trophies and splendors of their reign are commonwealths, rich in every attribute of great states, and united in a Republic whose power and prosperity and liberty and enlightment are the wonder and admiration of the world.

All hail, Columbus, discoverer, dreamer, hero, and apostle! We, here, of every race and country, recognize the horizon which bounded his vision and the infinite scope of his genius. The voice of gratitude and praise for all the blessings which have been showered upon mankind by his adventure is limited to no language, but is uttered in every tongue. Neither marble nor brass can fitly form his statue. Continents are his monument, and unnumbered millions present and to come, who enjoy in their liberties and their happiness the fruits of his faith, will reverently guard and preserve, from century to century, his name and fame.

Chauncey Mitchell Depew

AUTUMN

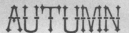

Autumn. A time when, early in the morning, the cool fog billows out over the lea, giving way to the dewdrops trickling down the ripe pumpkin that sits beneath the golden-brown corn stalks. Last night's frost ripened the apples which hang from sagging boughs; and a big, brown buck slowly browses the orchard, seeming to know autumn will not last long.

All this and more as we sight the cow-cropped fields to see the last aster waving chivalrously to Queen Anne's laced head. A final warm tempest blows the profuse fragrance of flowers in their zenith of genial power; and that sun that rose, lets fall its rays between the clouds to cast a radiant hue onto the leafed hills colored in gold, yellow, red, orange, and bits of evergreen.

Autumn. A time when the sky bustles with southerly action from the red-breasted robin to the multicolored ducks, and the sound of honkers fills the stilly air into the owly night. All moon long, the stars roll through the cirrus wisps high above the snow that had softly fallen through a silent night to cover the sown ground. And we awake to find the hush of nature's sleep.

Richard Dineen

The Robber's Gift

Florence S. Hallam

Robbers, as every child knows, are always sneaking, desperate men who, with hat pulled down over their eyes, and shoulders hunched against detection, lurk in darkness and in shadows. My robber was different. He had creases around his eyes that deepened when he smiled, and he wore a plaid jacket and a red scarf. What's more, he came in broad daylight.

He made his appearance during the depression years, when the big excitement in our house was the purchase of that newfangled concoction of batteries and dials called an Atwater Kent radio. We were more fortunate than most families because my father was working. His salary, though substantial enough to cover the mortgage payments on our one-family house in Spuyten Duyvil, a section of New York City, never stretched quite enough to accommodate the expenses of three growing daughters. Therefore, such a possession as a radio seemed like a dream, for its cost was unbelievable—over two hundred dollars! Yet one day, in a moment of weakness and longing, my usually sensible father succumbed to temptation and bought an Atwater Kent, nobly braving my mother's accusations of impracticality.

Evidentally, the radio's purchase was also noted by someone else. But that first week we felt only the wonderful glow of anticipation as we gathered nightly in our living room, with its overstuffed mohair sofa and matching armchair. Along with Mother, my two older sisters, and my eighty-six-year-old grandfather, I waited with a delicious tingle of anticipation, watching Dad perform the necessary magic rituals with the dials. Then, with incredible joy, we settled back and lost ourselves in that fascinating new world of "Amos 'n Andy." We also liked the songs of Ernie Jones and Billy Hare, the Happiness Boys, appearing for Loft's Candies. They would open with the song . . .

"If you like the way we chatter,
    With our songs and snappy patter,
Don't forget us when you know
    We're on the air!"

That first Saturday afternoon after the radio's arrival, I was surprised to see a car parked in front of our house. Rushing from play into our warm living room, I found a strange man kneeling by our radio, twisting the dials. Grandfather, in his high-backed Boston rocker, positioned to get the heat from the logs crackling in the fireplace, briefly left his world of reverie.

"Florrie," he said, fixing me with his cataract-filmed eyes, "This gentleman says he has to take our radio back to the store."

My ten-year-old world seemed to disintegrate as I regarded the nice young man who stopped his tinkering and rose to his feet.

"I'm doing a routine installation check on this set and I have to take it away. Trouble's too serious to fix here," he waved his arm at his car, parked outside.

"I told him," Grandfather said, "That he'd have to wait until your mother comes back."

I stretched my chilled hands toward the fire's warmth and turned sorrowful eyes toward the man.

"I hate to miss 'Orphan Annie'," I said. "She can't find Daddy Warbucks. Are you sure you can't fix it right here?"

"Will your mother be home soon?" he asked, shuffling his feet. "I have to be getting back."

"She's at the grocery store," I answered. "But you can use our phone to tell your store why you're taking so long."

Frowning, he shook his head and ran his fingers through his curly brown hair, which needed cutting.

"Would you like a nice, hot cup of cocoa while you're waiting?" Most people seemed to appreciate something to eat in those days; besides, my mother always made visitors a cup of tea, at least.

The man's blue eyes widened and he stared at me. "Ohhhhh, no, no! I don't want nothin', kid."

I went into the kitchen anyhow, and made three cups of cocoa, one for my grandfather, one for myself, and one for the man. When I tried to serve it, he drew away.

"Please take it," I implored. "It's awfully cold outside." Then, lowering my voice to a level that included him as my co-conspirator, I confided, "This is the kind of cocoa that Orphan Annie drinks. I only need one more label and they'll send me an Orphan Annie mug."

When he made no move to take it, I placed the cup and saucer on the lamp table beside him, and sat down on the other end of the sofa, drinking my cocoa.

The man looked at me for a long time. At least it seemed like a long time, but it was probably only a minute or so. It's strange, but I remember that look so clearly, even after all these years, because his gaze searched my face as though he had lost something and was trying to find it in my eyes.

Then he reached for his cup and gulped the cocoa so fast that I thought him a bit unmannerly. Abruptly, he thrust the empty cup into my hands.

"Think I'll have another look at that radio," he said, his voice kind of scratchy. Then he strode over and turned the dials while I watched him.

After a second or two he straightened up. "There, that should do it," he announced, his voice too loud. "Should have found that before. Loose coil. You'll be able to get your 'Orphan Annie' now," he said, hurrying into his plaid lumber jacket.

"Gosh," I said, "You didn't even have to turn the radio on. You must be a real good repairman."

"Yeah, kid." He gave me a funny, sad smile. "I'm a real good repairman," he answered, opening the front door.

Of course, when my father checked with the radio store he learned what he suspected, that the man was a fraud. They told Dad that if the man had taken the radio away we never would have seen it again.

In my childish innocence, I'd treated the thief as a fine, upright person; and for me he became one, if only for a short time. Remembering that, I've always tried to regard people as "good" not "bad," as "pleasant" not "nasty," and as "honest," rather than "dishonest." The result is, that in my lifetime, very few people have ever let me down.

For this, I must thank that thief. He left with me something infinitely more valuable than the radio that he didn't steal—a firm belief in the innate goodness of the human soul.

His Jack-O'-Lantern Smile

Joy Belle Burgess

Who is that up to his knees in leaves
In the thriving pumpkin patch?
It's my little boy in checkered sleeves
Looking for a jack-o'-lantern he can snatch!

He is thrilled at the sight of the speckled field,
Dotted with pumpkins ripe on the stems.
With arms clutching tight the best of its yield,
He carries off proudly a perfect-shaped gem!

He thinks of the goblins and ghosts he will scare
When he goes out spooking with "Jack" tonight.
Just wait until the witches with their straggly hair,
See "Jack's" eerie face and ride brooms out of sight!

He trudges down the path that leads to home,
Packing his pumpkin with the smooth orange skin.
As his shoes sink deep in the field's rich loam,
He muses on the fun he'll have when the night begins!

But later that day, why did he smile,
And show his daddy a toothless grin;
For with a knife in a very short while,
His daddy carved the pumpkin to look just like him!

It Was Halloween Eve at a Quarter-to-Four...

All week they've been cutting and pasting,
And Halloween trick-or-treats tasting;
But they won't eat a bite,
This Halloween night;
My children have no time for wasting.

As their mother I must say they're clever.
(Who, me? Slightly prejudiced? Never!)
This monster and witch
And ghost are a switch
From the usual costumes, however.

My ghost's a unique little fellow;
He insisted we dye his sheet yellow.
When we ran out of dye,
I gave one last try
And stained it with hot lemon Jell-o.

My monster evolved from green plastic,
(A garbage bag and some elastic.)
We emptied a box
And cut out some slots,
As the head it looks simply fantastic.

My poor little witch started crying
Because she had no broom for flying.
She managed to stop
When she spied the dust mop,
Which her quick-thinking dad was supplying.

Now off they go searching for treasure,
Which they'll eat later on at their leisure.
They knock on each door
And ask for some more
To fill their poor stomachs with pleasure.

Back home they come wearily creeping;
On the floor they leave trick-or-treats heaping;
They fall into bed;
I kiss each small head;
And soon, innocently, they're sleeping.

My creatures no longer look scary,
But next year I'll have to be wary
In helping each one
Prepare for the fun,
Which, I'm told, will involve something hairy.

Beverly Rae Wiersum

Halloween Treasure

One special night with darkened skies
On someone's porch a pumpkin lies.
The painted grin, so fierce and mean—
A pirate face for Halloween!

I must come closer, take a look
And see that Pumpkin Captain Hook.
I might be scared to see it there—
A pirate pumpkin's quite a scare!

Oh, wait! Not one, two, three, but four,
A gang of pirates at that door!
Four pirate pumpkins by a tree
In back, a ship upon a sea.

A clever artist made it so,
It looks so real, I'll have you know!
Four pumpkin pirates waiting there
To guard some treasure with great care.

The treasure, so much food to eat—
There's candy, gum balls—trick or treat!
I'll run right up and grab the goods,
Then hide the treasure in the woods.

But pirate pumpkins guard the chest.
I could take one and leave the rest!
A knife rests through one pirate's teeth.
He guards the candy spilled beneath.

A skull and crossbones on his head,
Another guards the candy bed.
I'm just too scared to take the treat.
I think I have what's called "cold feet"!

The third one winks an evil eye,
The fourth one stares and just stands by.
Those candies: red, green, blue, and white
Are guarded well by pirate fright!

But Halloween's for spooks like me,
Who like to get some treats for free.
So I'll just ring the bell to find
Who lives behind that door inside.

He might just tell me how to act,
To treat the pirates with great tact.
So I can take a piece or two—
To tell the truth, I'm scared right through!

Mary I. Schmal

Royal October

Oh! October the king of the months is here,
The hills in purple and gold appear;
His goldenrod scepter he holds on high
And he calls to the breezes that go rollicking by.

"Oh! winds tell the world I hold court these days
On the sun-kissed hills in the soft purple haze."
And his loving subjects haste at his call,
For they all rejoice at the voice of King Fall.

But Jack-in-the-Pulpit will come no more,
For an Indian in scarlet now stands in his door.
The trees turn red at the royal will,
And the blushing sumacs are on every hill.

The sweet fringed gentians from the lowlands nearby
Come in loveliest blue that vies with the sky,
And the asters in purple of every shade
Give a royal splendor to hill and glade.

The birches and maples in red and yellow
Stand brilliant and gorgeous in the sunshine mellow,
While the oaks' soft brown sometimes is seen
Burnt deepest red in splashes of green.

Oh! royal October all purple and gold!
Thy wealth and thy glory can never be told!
We bow to thy beauty, thy color, thy glow,
King October we love thee, we can't let thee go!

Louise B. Olmstead Jennings

Let me be
One with thee,
Riotous October!
Brown leaves dance,
Sunbeams glance,
Life is flowing over!

Where shall I
Find a sky
Softer, bluer, brighter?
Who has seen
Clouds that gleam
Airier and whiter?
Let me gaze
Through thy haze,
Misty month and sober.
Moods of gray,
Colors gay,
Both are thine, October.

Now all leaves,
Fruits and sheaves
Don their bright array;
And in state,
Celebrate
Nature's holiday.

Sister M. Albertina

Road to Autumn

Could this little old road be luring me now
  Deep into autumn's fold,
Through the glorious light of the noonday sun
  That illumines the trees of gold?

Through the vista that wanders and curves its way
  Along the dreaming hill;
Through a radiant wood of leaves and boughs
  That ring with the warblers' trill?

Could this little old road be enticing me now
  Through the Indian summer heat,
Where the meadows are sprawling with flowers and grass,
  And the orchard is mellow-sweet?

Where the faraway hill stirs and glistens anew
  In the beautiful autumn glow?
Could this little old road be beckoning now . . .
  My heart is eager, and I must go!

Joy Belle Burgess

Something Told the Wild Geese

Something told the wild geese
It was time to go.
Though the fields lay golden
Something whispered, "Snow."
Leaves were green and stirring,
Berries, luster-glossed,
But beneath warm feathers
Something cautioned, "Frost."
All the sagging orchards
Steamed with amber spice,
But each wild breast stiffened
At remembered ice.
Something told the wild geese
It was time to fly—
Summer sun was on their wings,
Winter in their cry.

Rachel Field

Autumn Oracle

A sunset sky, and the west wind sighing,
A threat of winter . . . the wild gulls crying;
Swift flocks of birds to the southland winging;
Bare brown boughs in a frenzy flinging
Dying leaves that for long were holden,
Now drifting, dropping, crimson and golden.
The fallen leaves, in uncounted number,
Are warmly quilting the wildflower's slumber;
There are buds on the bough . . . a springtime presage . . .
The birds will return with a lyric message;
The wild gull's cry holds a hint of mating,
To conquer cold is the hearthfire waiting.
The west wind's sighs are of love, not sorrow,
And the sunset sky is the sign for tomorrow.

Laura Lee Randall

Winter's Call

Silently it claims the earth,
Touching leaf and craggy bark
With softness.

Gentle flakes sifting down
To drape in filmy clinging lace
Each nook and sylvan scene,
Nature's jewel case.

Crystal teardrops caught in sunbeams,
Strands of pearls etch the sky.
Diamonds pinpoint earthly settings,
Heavenly beauty lights the eye.

Muffled now the wild bird's call,
The wandering stream sings no more;
Muted golds, reds, and wintery green
Reflecting from its silvery sheen.

Autumn's heady, wine-like air
Turns misty, cool
All nature stilled, bows low,
In the hush of winter's call.

Joan C. Callahan

Joy Belle Burgess

Joy Belle Burgess loves nature and the out-of-doors, a fact which stems from being raised on a farm outside Portland, Oregon. Behind the farm stretched a rippling stream and timber-covered mountain which she loved to visit. Being an only child, her various pets were her most frequent companions, a fact which makes her fondly recall of her parents, "I had a very understanding and kind mother and father." Mrs. Burgess, while raising a family of six children, has been actively involved in civic volunteer services in which she worked for the passage of a county library levy, supported programs urging youth involvement, and participated in her local PTA. Mrs. Burgess is not only a volunteer civic worker, but she has nearly completed her second four-year term as elected city council-woman for Milwaukie, Oregon. In spite of a busy home and political life, Mrs. Burgess still finds time for her best-loved hobby—poetry, of which she says, "I find a most wonderful satisfaction and peace of mind in isolating myself from the world, meditating upon deep, inspiring, uplifting thoughts and painting scenes with colorful, rhyming, depictive words and phrases." Through poetry, Joy Belle Burgess finds respite from the practical world of home and politics.

Autumn Glory

Oh, the glorious days of autumn,
When the trees wear flowing robes,
And glisten in the sunlight,
Full-orbed in autumn's glow!

O'er the slopes and rolling hillside,
The tall and stately evergreens
Interweave their graceful boughs
Into the ever-changing scenes.

Into the days of flaming glory
As autumn gathers in her fold
Jewels that glisten in the sunlight,
Leaves of crimson, brown and gold.

Oh, the days of glowing splendor,
When Nature waves her magic wand,
The vivid trees that grace the forest
Fill the hills with autumn's song!

Hillside of Gold

Let me follow the rise of the meadow
Where it rims the far-flung sky,
Above the lingering haze of the valley
To the brow of a hill most high;
For sweet is the call to come hither
And be enveloped in autumn's fold,
To walk in its glow and splendor
Up the shining hillside of gold.

Let me follow the way to the woodland
Where the boughs glow yellow and brown,
Where trees fling their shower of gold
And bright-spangled wealth to the ground;
Where the sky is a whirlwind of yellow
Aglow with the frolicking leaves,
And joy is newborn with each trill
That floats on the autumn breeze.

Let me climb to the brow of the hill
Where the air is fragrant and sweet,
Where the rich, gleaming jewels of the frost
Lay a carpet of gold at my feet;
For still, there's a call to come hither
And watch the beauty of autumn unfold;
To tarry . . . and treasure each moment . . .
On the shining hillside of gold.

Autumn Trail

The trail is a ribbon of sunlight
That meanders through the trees,
Fringed by the boughs of autumn
And kissed by the falling leaves;
A way unrolled before me
Wending deep into autumn's fold
Where the wondrous world of beauty
Is waiting for me to behold.

The woods are ablaze with color
Along the trail's domain
Where I tremble beneath the glow
Of maples wrapped in fiery flames,
And I cannot quench the flares
Resplendent with yellow light . . .
The aspens in their glistening robes
That ever glow more bright.

The Covered Bridge

This covered bridge, quaint and weatherworn,
Still lends its dignity and charm
To the quiet little country road
That winds past meadowland and farm.
And within the stream's full melody
That echoes against its darkened walls,
It hears the tramplings of a yeasteryear
Faintly above the waters' splash and fall.

And still resound the clopping hooves
Against its heavy planks;
The creaking wheels of loaded carts,
And laughter along the sun-drenched banks.
Even yet it heeds the low sweet song
Of a bygone day's rememberings,
When a swaying haycart left its drifts
And farmers tarried to talk of crops and things.

This covered bridge, quaint and weatherworn,
Still stands with dignity and charm,
Though its split and seasoned timbers
Shelter only blackbirds that fly tween field and farm.
And glints of sunlight are all that move
Across its timeworn planks . . . but still it hears
Above the waters' splash and fall,
Faint echoings of long-remembered years.

Jewels in the Sun

Now every leaf that glistens
Is a jewel in the sun
Along the wooded byway
Where autumn's wealth is flung.

The treasures glow and mingle
On boughs above the lane,
Where poplars cast their yellow flare
And maples lift their flame.

The leaves are steeped in sunlight
And ruffled by a breeze
That stirs within their golden maze
And whispers through the trees.

And the autumn sky is brimming
With colors to behold . . .
With leaves that glide and nestle deep
Into a carpeting of gold.

How warmly now the earth enfolds
Her treasures one by one,
The lane is bright, more deeply full,
With jewels in the sun.

Ideals' Pages
from the Past

On the following six pages
we are presenting a selection
from Autumn Ideals 1952.

Autumn Night

Mildred P. Van Horn

When days and nights near equal lengths
And warm day-winds lie down to die,
The waxing moon begins to paint
Its orange-gold across the sky.

The bottom lands grow powder-gray
With mists that travel in the night,
And birds cry out against the chill
Which starts the migratory flight.

The rail fence staggers with a load
Of clutching vines in purple capes;
The chill night air is keenly sweet
And fragrant with wild frosty grapes.

As night slips on her mystic gown
And all the woodsy things creep forth,
Far in the blue-black sky above
The dipper lies low in the north.

As dark pines lift green fingers up
To turn on all the silver lights,
The loveliness of plum-ripe days
Is changed to autumn's bracing nights.

Fall Plowing

Grace Noll Crowell

The grain is reaped and threshed and gone,
   And only the stubble remaining now;
And there in a great field tramps a team
   And a man is riding a plow.

Over and over the long rows lift,
   Sweetly smelling, and moist, and brown,
The damp earth turned to the wind and sun,
   And the stubble gold turned down.

Up the length of the field and back,
   Across the width of a lessening square,
Around and around from morning until
   The noon sun strikes them there.

A brief hour spent at table and trough,
   Then out to the field again they go—
And man, and the team, and the steel-sharp plow,
   And the darkening furrows grow.

Something there is of Faith that shines
   Over a field of an autumn day;
Something of trust and of steadfast hope,
   Follows a plowman's way.

Faith in the year that is to come,
   Trust in the Giver of sun and rain,
Hope that up from the torn dark rows
   There shall spring other grain.

The Farmer

Ethel Romig Fuller

He needs no calendar, no clock,
Who rises with the crowing cock;
Who goes to bed, his long day done,
With the robins and the sun;

Whose seasons are determined by
Conditions of the ground and sky:
Spring, when catkins on a bough
And frogs proclaim the hour to plow.

Summer, suddenly a day
Redolent with new-mown hay,
And lyrical with rustling wheat
Heading yellow in the heat.

Autumn—maples turning red,
Wild geese honking overhead—
A time to pilfer apple trees,
Sack hickory nuts, hold husking bees.

Winter — scarlet muffler donned —
Ice for the cutting in a pond;
And oaks to topple in the chill,
Snow-drifted woodlot on a hill:

He, whose time-piece tells the hours
By rain and drought, by frost and flowers;
He, to whom the seasons are
A variable, bright calendar.

Let Gratitude Compare

David Murray

Nature does not economize;
　She gives with lavish hand.
She knows not what meanness is
　In sky, on sea or land.

One half the stars we see at night
　Would deck a royal bride.
But millions twinkle ever bright,
　With millions more beside.

The mighty oceans yield their store
　Of fishes large and small;
The harvest there is ever ripe —
　At man's eternal call.

Half the blossoms on the chestnut
　Would be something to admire.
Nature's cup still overflows —
　With beauty does conspire.

Let gratitude within our hearts
　With nature's gifts compare,
And praise the Hand that nobly gives
　Abundance, and to spare.

Page opposite
THE WHEATFIELD
Leon L'Hermitte
(1844–1925)
Museum of Fine Arts, Boston

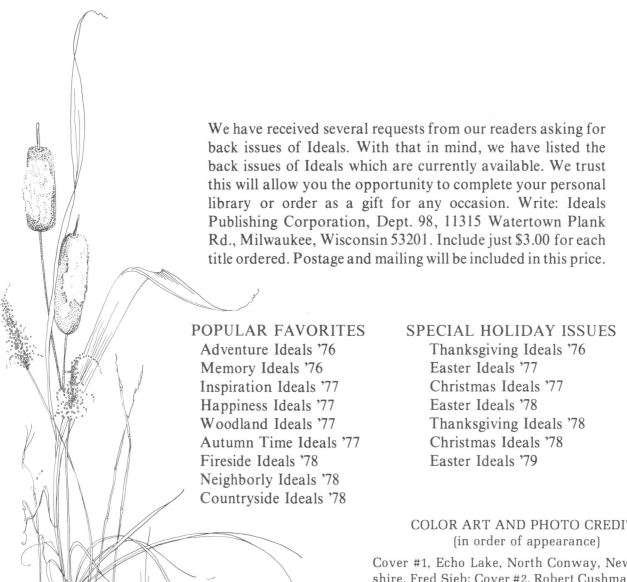

We have received several requests from our readers asking for back issues of Ideals. With that in mind, we have listed the back issues of Ideals which are currently available. We trust this will allow you the opportunity to complete your personal library or order as a gift for any occasion. Write: Ideals Publishing Corporation, Dept. 98, 11315 Watertown Plank Rd., Milwaukee, Wisconsin 53201. Include just $3.00 for each title ordered. Postage and mailing will be included in this price.

POPULAR FAVORITES
Adventure Ideals '76
Memory Ideals '76
Inspiration Ideals '77
Happiness Ideals '77
Woodland Ideals '77
Autumn Time Ideals '77
Fireside Ideals '78
Neighborly Ideals '78
Countryside Ideals '78

SPECIAL HOLIDAY ISSUES
Thanksgiving Ideals '76
Easter Ideals '77
Christmas Ideals '77
Easter Ideals '78
Thanksgiving Ideals '78
Christmas Ideals '78
Easter Ideals '79

COLOR ART AND PHOTO CREDITS
(in order of appearance)

Cover #1, Echo Lake, North Conway, New Hampshire, Fred Sieb; Cover #2, Robert Cushman Hayes; East Topsham, Vermont, Fred M. Dole; Back to school, Fred Sieb; Apple orchard, Door County, Wisconsin, Ken Dequaine; Red Eagle Pond, Conway, New Hampshire, Fred Sieb; Peacham, Vermont, Freelance Photographers Guild; Weston, Vermont, Alpha Photo, Inc.; Autumn splendor, Fred Sieb; The burning of the leaves, Eric M. Sanford; Victorian glass, H. Russell Zimmermann; Owens Valley, California, Josef Muench; Cadillac Mts., Acadia National Park, Maine, Ed Cooper; Alaskan bear, Rollie Ostermick; Cumbria, Lake Windermere, England, Colour Library International (USA) Limited; Basket of chrysanthemums, Gerald Koser; Near Leland, Wisconsin, Ken Dequaine; Gathering pumpkins, Freelance Photographers Guild; Pirate's Halloween, Gerald Koser; Autumn road, Freelance Photographers Guild; First snowfall, Pinkham Notch, New Hampshire, Fred Sieb; Country road in autumn, J. I. Greenleaf; THE WHEATFIELD, Leon L'Hermitte (1844-1925), Museum of Fine Arts, Boston; Cover #3, Alpha Photo, Inc.; Cover #4, Albany, New Hampshire, Alpha Photo, Inc.

ACKNOWLEDGMENTS
A LOVE OF BEAUTY by George Matthew Adams. Copyright. Used by permission of The Washington Star Syndicate, Inc. AN AUTUMN LANDSCAPE by Grace Noll Crowell. Used by permission of Reid Crowell. THE TASTE OF FRESHLY-MADE MOLASSES by Ruth Straight Hibbs. Reprinted with permission of FARM WIFE NEWS magazine. Our sincere thanks to the following authors whose addresses we were unable to locate: Cecil Brown for THE OLD HOMETOWN; James L. Hughes for AUTUMN'S FAIRYLAND; Louise B. Olmstead Jennings for OH, OCTOBER THE KING . . . ; Laura Lee Randall for AUTUMN ORACLE.